I Can Do It Myself

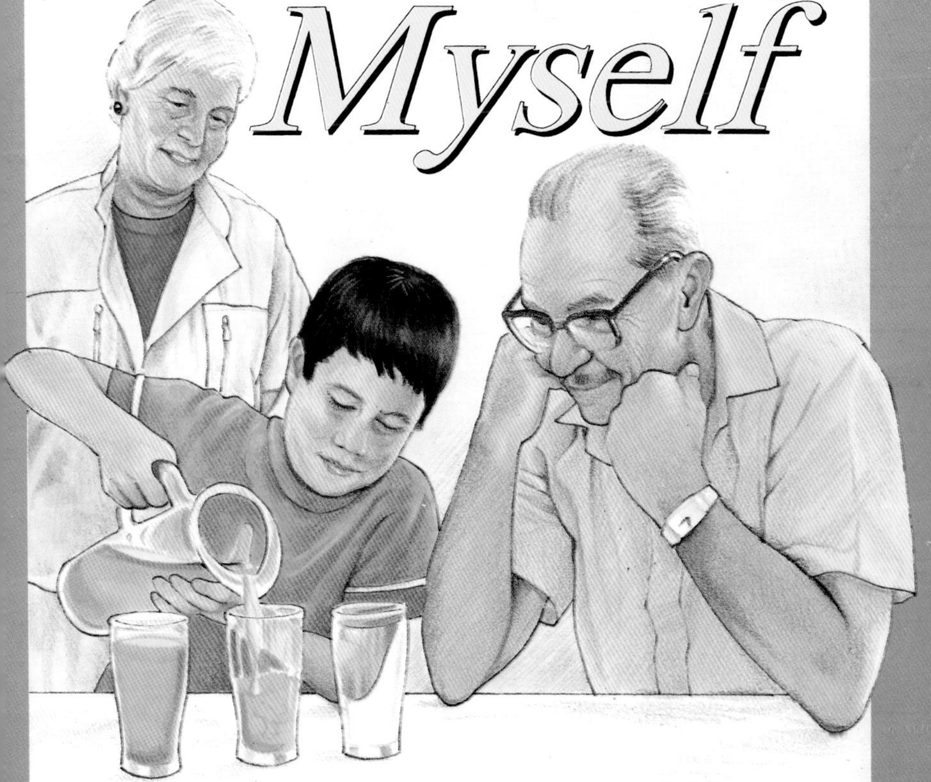

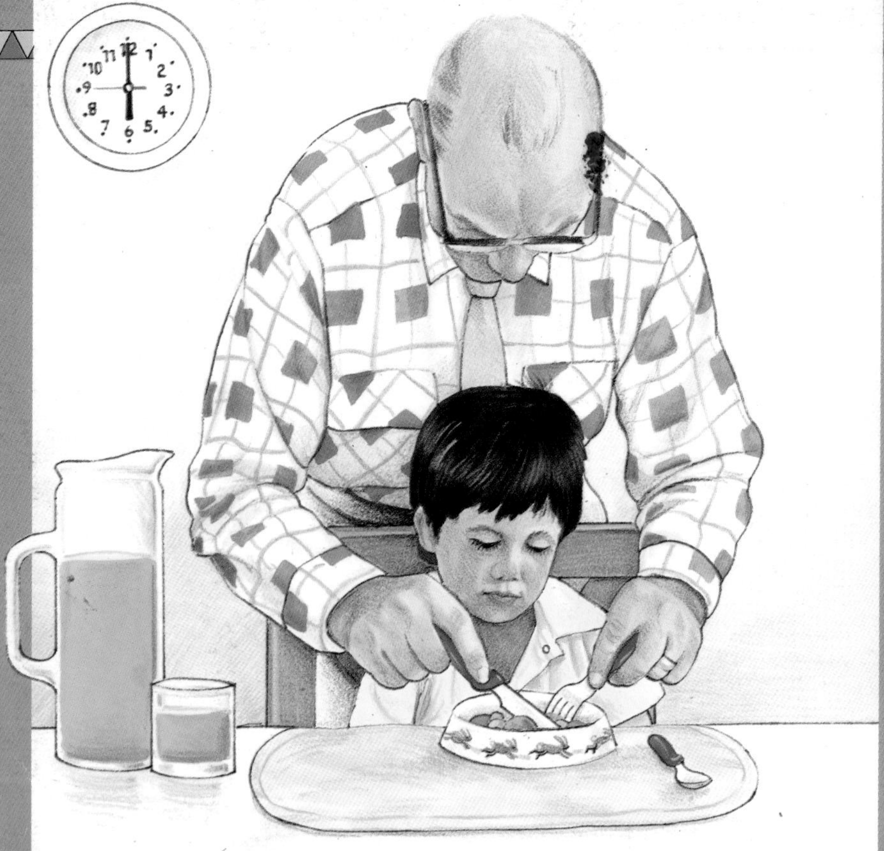

Grandpa used to cut up my food.

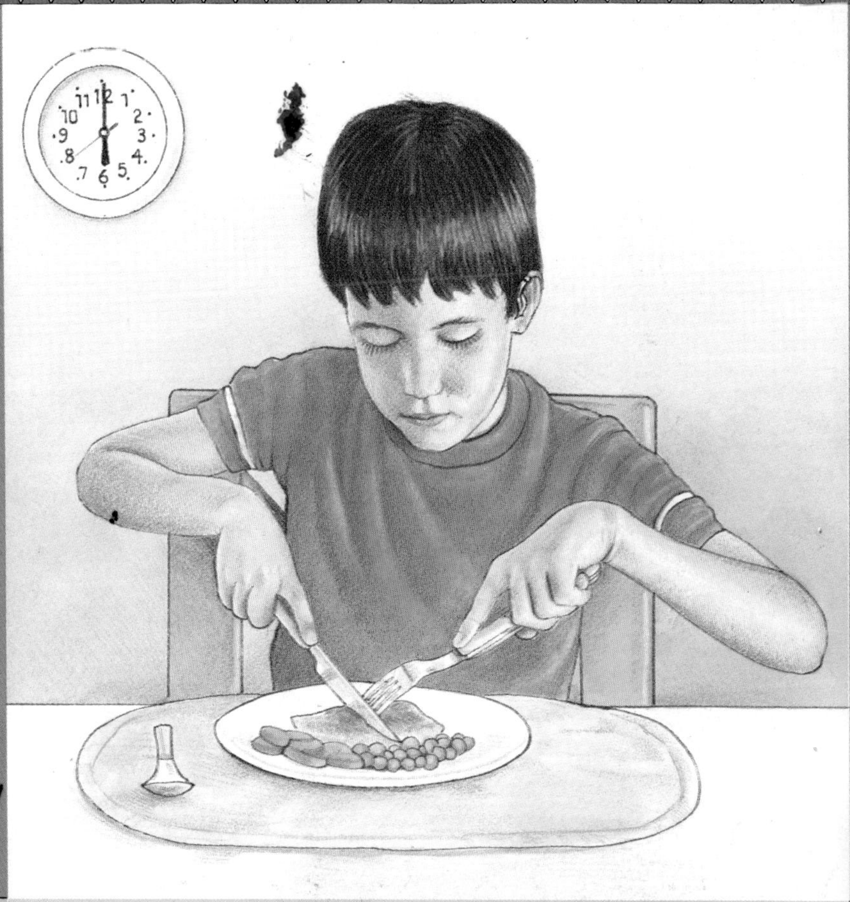

Now I can do it myself.

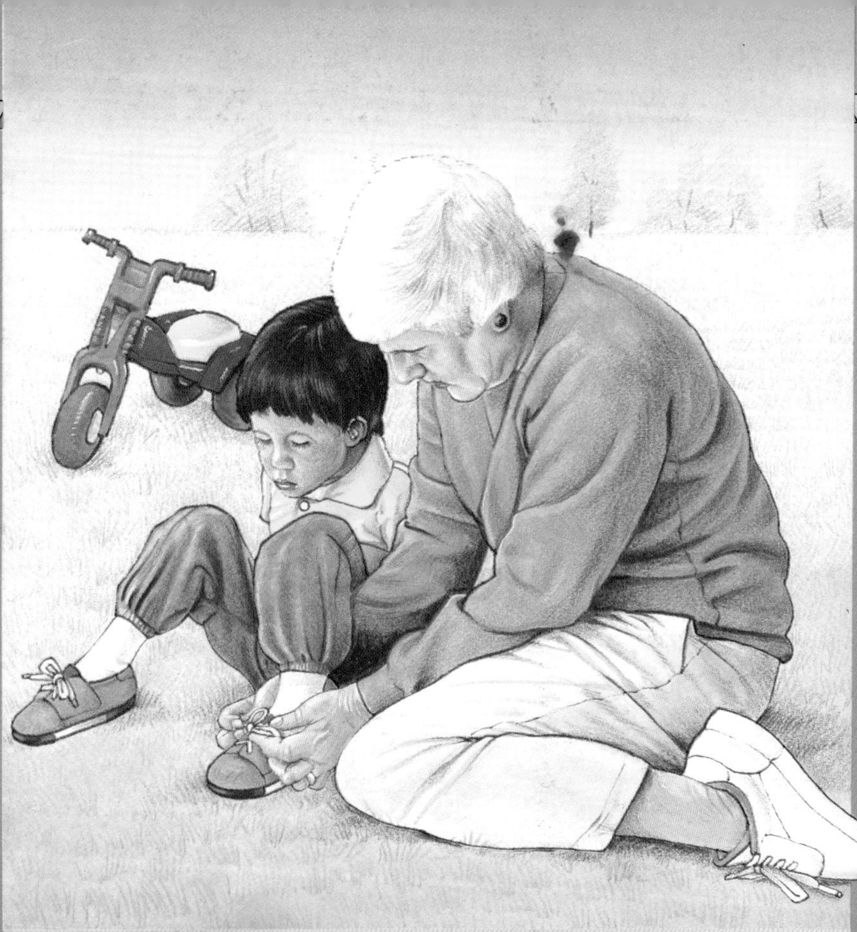

Grandma used to tie my shoes.

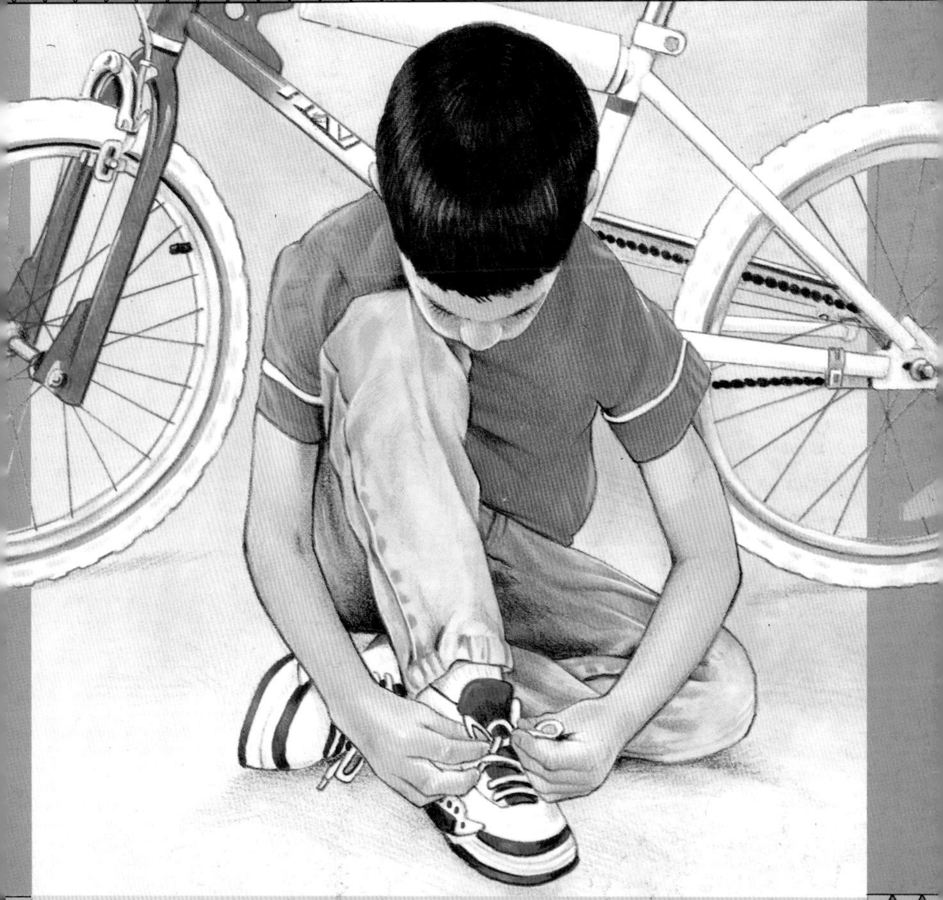

Now I can do it myself.

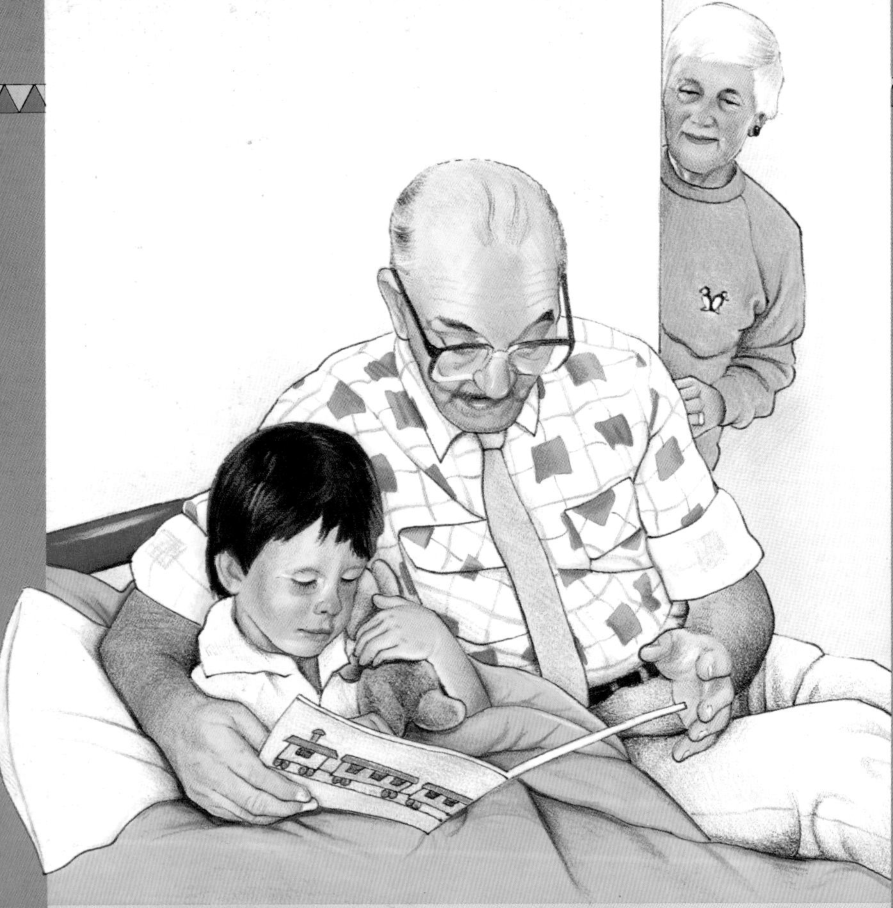

Grandpa used to read me stories.

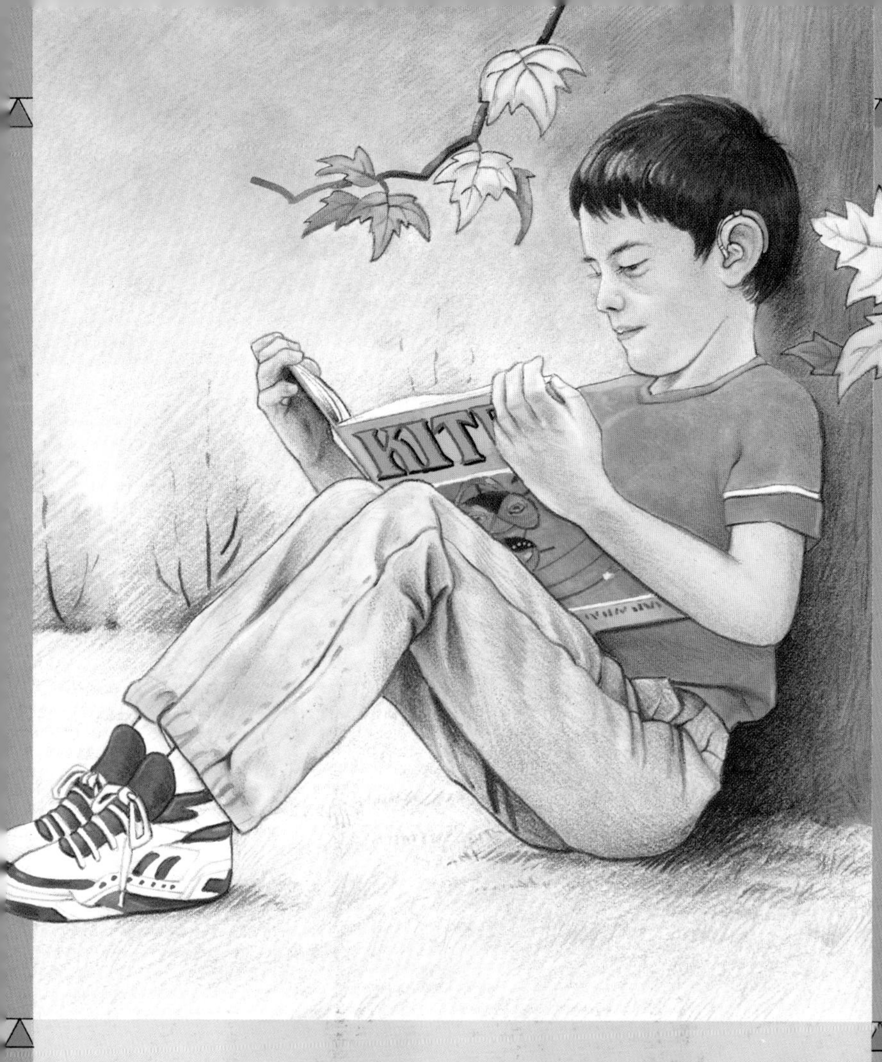

Now I can do it myself.

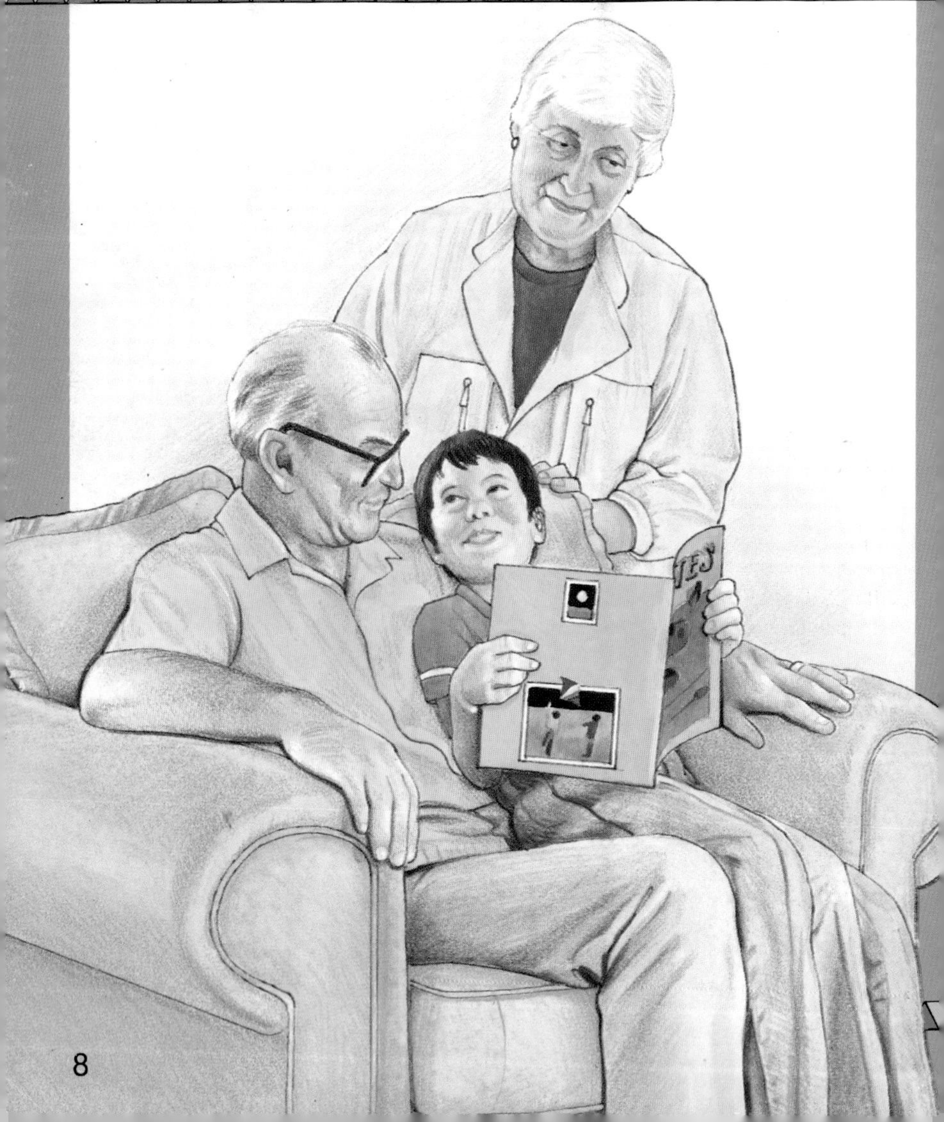

TES